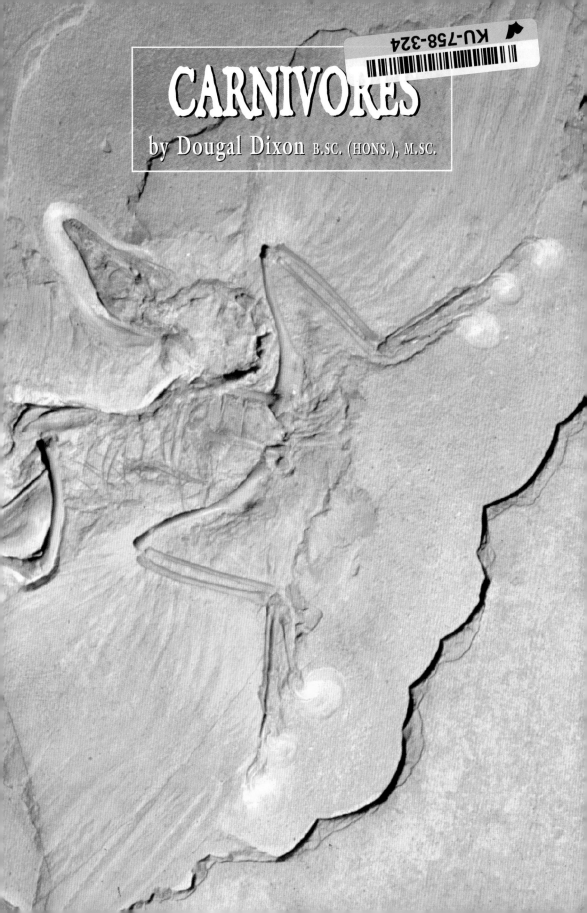

CARNIVORES

by Dougal Dixon B.SC. (HONS.), M.SC.

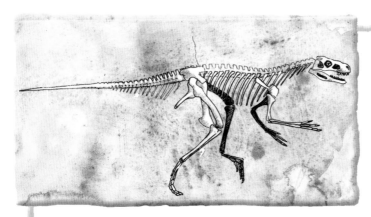

POWERFUL LEGS

A meat-eating dinosaur, *Herrerasaurus* walked on strong hind legs, with its teeth and the claws on its arms held out to the front where they could do most damage. The back was held horizontally and the body was balanced by a long tail. This set the pattern for all meat-eating dinosaurs to come.

BEFORE THE DINOSAURS

During the Permian period, the main plant-eating animals of the time were mammal-like reptiles. They had teeth like mammals, and some were even hairy. The biggest were built like hippopotami, such as the broad-headed *Moschops* shown here. At the same time as the first dinosaurs evolved, the first mammals evolved too. Descended from the mammal-like reptiles, they were small and furry and bore live young. If the dinosaurs had not come to prominence, the mammals may well have taken over. Instead, they had to wait 160 million years before they evolved into anything important.

EORAPTOR

Eoraptor was about the size of a fox and, like all the dinosaurs to follow, walked on legs that were held straight under the body. This made it a much faster animal than the other reptiles that walked on legs sprawled out to the side.

TIGER-SIZED

Herrerasaurus was a much bigger animal than *Eoraptor*, about the size of a tiger. One of the first dinosaurs, it was a primitive theropod, part of the group that includes all the meat-eaters. Adults could reach a length of 3 metres (10 ft). The skeleton of a *Herrerasaurus* was found in Argentina, in South America.

WHERE DID THEY COME FROM?

Dinosaurs! The most famous of all extinct animals, the whale-sized reptiles that dominated the Earth for about 160 million years. Reptiles evolved during the Carboniferous period, about 350 million years ago, and flourished during the succeeding Permian, Triassic, Jurassic and Cretaceous periods. During this Age of Reptiles, there were land-living reptiles, swimming reptiles, flying reptiles, herbivores (plant-eaters), carnivores (meat-eaters) and omnivores (both plant and meat-eaters) – reptiles of all kinds in every environment. At the end of the Cretaceous era, about 65 million years ago, all the big reptiles died out and mammals took over. The Age of Reptiles was well under way before the first dinosaurs appeared around the end of the Triassic period, 225 million years ago.

EORAPTOR SKULL

An x-ray photograph of *Eoraptor's* skull shows how its lightweight skull was made up of thin struts of bone. The dinosaur's light bone structure enabled it to move fast. The skulls of most subsequent meat-eating dinosaurs were built like this.

RAUISUCHIAN

Before the dinosaurs came along, the biggest of the hunters were a group of land-living crocodile relatives called rauisuchians. They had big heads and many sharp teeth and, although they were slow-moving, they were faster than the plant-eating reptiles that abounded at the time.

CARBONIFEROUS 360-286 MYA	PERMIAN 286-248 MYA	TRIASSIC 245-208 MYA	EARLY/MID JURASSIC 208-157 MYA	LATE JURASSIC 157-146 MYA

LIKE MEGALOSAURUS?

For a long time, the name *Megalosaurus* was applied to the fossil of any meat-eating dinosaur found in Britain or Europe. All kinds of unrelated dinosaurs were erroneously given the name. Only now is this mess of different animals being sorted out. There is a virtually complete skeleton of *Eustreptospondylus* in the Oxford University Museum in England. This was one of the dinosaurs once thought to be a *Megalosaurus*.

MEGALOSAURUS JAW

The lower jawbone and teeth of *Megalosaurus* were the first parts of the animal to be discovered. They were found in Oxfordshire, England, in about 1815. The Reverend William Buckland studied them and deduced from the sharp pointed teeth that they had belonged to a meat-eating animal, and that it had been a large reptile. Other scientists studied the remains in the 1820s and one of them – history does not tell us who – came up with the name *Megalosaurus*.

FIRST DINOSAUR THEME PARK

Because of the great public interest in science in the mid-nineteenth century, part of Crystal Palace park in South London was developed as an ancient landscape. Statues (which still stand today) were erected showing the three dinosaurs and the marine reptiles that were known at the time. All that was known of *Megalosaurus* was its jawbone, teeth and a few fragments of bone. Since nobody knew what the animal actually looked like, it was modelled as a fearsome four-footed dragon-like creature.

| TRIASSIC 245-208 MYA | EARLY/MID JURASSIC 208-157 MYA | LATE JURASSIC 157-146 MYA | EARLY CRETACEOUS 146-97 MYA | LATE CRETACEOUS 97-65 MYA |

THE FIRST KNOWN

Since civilization began, people have known about giant bones embedded in the rocks. In earliest times they were spoken of in legends as the bones of giants and dragons and other mythical creatures. By the early nineteenth century, however, scientific knowledge had advanced sufficiently for scientists to begin to appreciate the true nature of fossils. In 1842, the British anatomist, Sir Richard Owen, invented the term 'dinosauria' (terrible lizards) to classify three fossil animals whose skeletons had been discovered in England during the previous two decades. One was the plant-eating *Iguanodon*, which is now quite well known. Another was the armoured *Hylaeosaurus*, which we still know very little about. The first of the trio to be brought to light and described was the carnivorous *Megalosaurus*.

WILLIAM BUCKLAND (1784–1856)

This nineteenth century clergyman was typical of his time. When not in the pulpit he spent his extensive spare time doing scientific research. Most of the fossils he studied were those of sea-living animals – seashells and marine reptiles. Fossils of land-living animals have always been more rare (*see page 32*). He may not have invented the name *Megalosaurus* but he was the scholar who did all the scientific work on it.

MODERN VIEW

Even today, we do not have a clear idea of what *Megalosaurus* looked like because so few fossilized remains have been found. Like all meat-eating dinosaurs, it must have walked on its hind legs with its big head held well forward, balanced by a heavy tail. Fossils found in lagoon deposits in what is now Normandy in northern France suggest that *Megalosaurus* was a shoreline scavenger that prowled along the beach, eating the dead things that had been washed up.

EARLY HUNTERS

Most of the early meat-eating dinosaurs were small animals, some no bigger than our domestic cats and dogs. They probably fed mainly on even smaller animals, such as lizards and the early mammals. However, most of the plant-eating reptiles of the time were quite large animals and would also have made good prey for the meat-eaters. Some of the early dinosaurs adopted a strategy of hunting in packs so that they could bring down and kill some of these big plant-eaters. Today, such team-work is still used in the wild by animals such as Canadian wolves, which hunt moose much bigger than themselves. Similarly, on the African plains, groups of hyenas attack wildebeest that are far bigger than they are.

THE CONNECTICUT FOOTPRINTS

At the beginning of the nineteenth century, long before anybody knew anything about dinosaurs, farmers in New England, USA, kept finding three-toed trackways in the Triassic sandstone at the foot of the Appalachian Mountains, shown above. At first, it was believed the footprints were made by giant birds that had existed in the area before Noah's flood as described in the Bible. We now know they were footprints of dinosaur packs, probably made by *Coelophysis* or something similar.

TRIASSIC	EARLY/MID JURASSIC	LATE JURASSIC	EARLY CRETACEOUS	LATE CRETACEOUS
245-208 MYA	208-157 MYA	157-146 MYA	146-97 MYA	97-65 MYA

BIRD & DINOSAUR FOOTPRINTS

Birds and dinosaurs are so closely related it is little wonder the footprints of one could be mistaken for those of the other. In a series of ridges of Jurassic and Cretaceous rocks in the flanks of the Rocky Mountains west of Denver, USA, there are fossilized footprints of both dinosaurs and birds. Bird footprints can be distinguished from dinosaur prints by the greater spread of their toes – about 90° as opposed to about 45°. There is also often a trace of the little fourth toe pointing backwards. In dinosaurs, this toe is usually well clear of the ground.

DINOSAUR   BIRD

ONE WORLD

In late Triassic and early Jurassic times the world was very different from the way it is today. All the continental landmasses were joined together in one area, called Pangaea. Since there was only one landmass, animals of the same kind were able to migrate everywhere. This is why we find the remains of almost identical animals in New Mexico and Connecticut, USA, as well as in Zimbabwe, thousands of miles away on the African continent.

SYNTARSUS

In 1972, a remarkable deposit of fossils was found in Rhodesia (now Zimbabwe). A mass of bones lay in fine river sediment, sandwiched between rocks formed from sand dunes. The fossils were of a pack of small meat-eating dinosaurs of different sizes and ages. They seemed to have drowned in a flash flood that struck as they were crossing a dry river bed. These meat-eating dinosaurs, named *Syntarsus*, were almost identical in build to *Coelophysis* and some scientists think they were a species of the same animal.

COELOPHYSIS

Late Triassic *Coelophysis* was a 3-metre (10-ft) long carnivore. In the 1940s, a whole group of them was discovered fossilized in New Mexico, evidently having perished in a drought. Since they had both lived and died together, it was deduced that these animals moved about in packs or family groups. Another behavioural trait came to light when the skeleton of a youngster was found in the stomach area of one of the adults. Perhaps they had been so desperate for food that they ate their own kind.

CREST-HEADED BEASTS

Look at the bright colours of many birds – the long tail feathers of a peacock, the gaudy bill of a toucan, the red breast of a robin. Colour is part of a bird's method of communication. Their brain can 'read' the colours they see and enables them to recognize whether another bird is a friend or foe. Birds are related to dinosaurs (*see pages 20–21*), which had similar brains and senses. It is very likely that dinosaurs also used colour for communication. Some dinosaurs (especially among the carnivores) had crests and horns as brightly coloured as the plumage of modern birds.

DILOPHOSAURUS IN LIFE

In life, *Dilophosaurus* probably looked dazzling. It seems very likely that its crests were particula colourful either to frighten rivals or attract a mate from far away. The rest of the animal m also have been brightly coloured to back up the signals given by the crests. Dewlaps (fla of skin beneath the chin) may have been brightly coloured like modern lizards, a would also have been part of the displ

FORWARD THINKING

The early Jurassic meat-eater from Antarctica, *Cryolophosaurus*, had a crest that curled up and forwards above its eyes. The bony core was probably covered in brightly-coloured horn or skin. *Cryolophosaurus* is the only dinosaur known to have had a crest that ran across the skull rather than along it. At 8 metres (26 ft) long, it was probably the biggest meat-eater of its time, its size enhanced still further by the crest.

HORNED MONSTER

In the late Jurassic, one of the fiercest of the dinosaurs was *Ceratosaurus*, 6 metres (20 ft) long. It lived in North America and Tanzania in East Africa. *Ceratosaurus* had a heavy head with a horn on the nose and another pair of horns above the eyes. The heavy skull suggests they may have fought with one another by head-battering, but the horns were very lightly built and would not have been much use as weapons. They may have been used only for display, and perhaps only the males had them for courtship rituals.

MONOLOPHOSAURUS

The crest of *Monolophosaurus*, a medium-sized middle Jurassic meat-eating dinosaur from China, was made up of a pair of skull bones fused together and growing upwards. Air gaps and channels between these bones were connected to the nostrils and may have been used to amplify grunts and roars generated in the animal's throat. In this way the crest would have helped it communicate by sound as well as visually.

DILOPHOSAURUS SKELETON

Dilophosaurus was a bear-sized, meat-eating dinosaur from the early Jurassic of North America. The first skeleton found had semicircular plate-like structures lying near it. Later finds showed that these structures were crests that ran parallel to one another along the length of the skull. However, what no skeleton can ever tell us is what colour the crests were in life.

| TRIASSIC 245-208 MYA | EARLY/MID JURASSIC 208-157 MYA | LATE JURASSIC 157-146 MYA | EARLY CRETACEOUS 146-97 MYA | LATE CRETACEOUS 97-65 MYA |

HEAVY CLAW

Baryonyx was discovered by an amateur fossil collector in southern England in 1983. The skeleton was so complete that it gave us the first clear view of what these animals looked like. *Baryonyx* was an unusual meat-eating dinosaur that had crocodile-like jaws packed with sharp teeth, and long forelimbs with hooked claws, which were used to catch fish.

Baryonyx **stood 3 metres (10 ft) tall, and each of its claws measured nearly 35 cm (12 inches) long. It probably ranged over a large area stretching from England to North Africa.**

SPINOSAURUS

MENACING MIMIC

Suchomimus was found in a remote dune-covered area of the Sahara in 1998 by a team from the United States and Niger. An enormous predatory dinosaur with a skull like a crocodile's and huge thumb claws, it measured 11 metres (36 ft) in length and 4 metres (12 ft) high at the hip. The thumb claws and powerfully built forelimbs were used to snare prey, and the thin sail along its back, which reached a height of half a metre (2 ft) over the hips, may have been brightly coloured for display.

SPINOSAURUS - 15 metres (50 ft) long, 7 metres (24 ft) high
SUCHOMIMUS - 11 metres (36 ft) long, 4 metres (12 ft high)
BARYONYX - 10 metres (32 ft) long, 3 metres (10 ft) high
IRRITATOR - 6 metres (21 ft) long, 2 metres (6 ft) high

BARYONYX

BIG BITE

Many modern reptiles have similarities to the spinosaurids. Crocodiles and alligators, for example, have long jaws and many teeth, and hunt for fish in a similar way. Like the spinosaurids, they were both for a long time wrongly suspected of eating their young.

SPINOSAURIDS - THE FISH EATERS

We normally think of fish-eating animals as creatures that live in the water. However, there are many land-living animals that like to take fish too. Grizzly bears are often seen beside waterfalls hooking out migrating salmon as they leap up to their spawning grounds, and otters live mostly on land but hunt fish. It was the same in the Jurassic period. One particular family of land-dwelling dinosaurs – the spinosaurids – seem to have been particularly well-equipped for fishing. They had long jaws with many small teeth, and a big claw on each hand. They lived in early Cretaceous times, and their remains have been found across the world, from Southern England to North Africa and South America.

SUCHOMIMUS

IRRITATOR

SPINY CUSTOMER

Spinosaurus was excavated in Egypt in 1915. Unfortunately, its remains were destroyed when its museum in Germany was bombed in World War II. What we do know about it was that it was as big as *Tyrannosaurus* and had a fin down its back, almost two metres (6½ ft) tall. The fin was probably used to cool the animal in hot weather. In 1999, an American expedition found its original quarry in Egypt, so there may be hope of finding new specimens in the future.

HERE'S ONE I MADE EARLIER

Irritator was given its name because of the confusing circumstances in which it was found. The skull – all that we have of the animal – was collected in Brazil sometime in the 1990s and sent to the museum in Stuttgart, Germany. But then the museum staff had a surprise. Whoever dug it up and sold it to the museum had added pieces to it and stuck it together with car body filler to make it look much more spectacular. Now that we have had a proper look at it, we can tell that it is a small spinosaurid.

TRIASSIC 245-208 MYA	EARLY/MID JURASSIC 208-157 MYA	LATE JURASSIC 157-146 MYA	EARLY CRETACEOUS 146-97 MYA	LATE CRETACEOUS 97-65 MYA

NQWEBASAURUS

Scientists became very excited in the late 1990s when they found the almost complete skeleton of one-metre (3-ft) long *Nqwebasaurus* embedded in early Cretaceous rocks in South Africa. It proved that the family to which most of the small meat-eating dinosaurs belonged (the coelurosaurids) had existed in the southern continents during the Cretaceous period, as well as in North America, Europe and Asia.

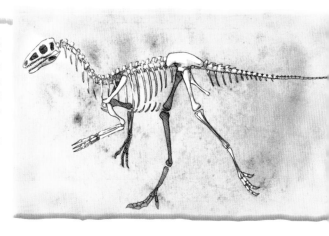

ITALIAN BEAUTY

In the 1990s, this beautifully-preserved skeleton of *Scipionyx* was found in early Cretaceous rocks in Italy. It was so finely fossilized, even some of the soft anatomy (the lungs and guts) were preserved. Their existence confirms that this animal, probably along with all other small dinosaurs, was able to breathe efficiently while running. This would have made it an energetic and active hunter. The way the bones were articulated indicate that this specimen of *Scipionyx*, only 25 cm (10 inches) long, was not yet fully grown.

TINIEST FOOTPRINT

In the 1970s, the tiny footprint of a dinosaur that could have been no bigger than a thrush was found in the late Triassic rocks of Newfoundland in Canada. The arrangement of the toes is typical of the meat-eating dinosaurs of the Triassic. The print is the only trace we have of the smallest dinosaur ever found. Whether it was a youngster or fully grown, nobody yet knows.

THE SMALLEST DINOSAURS

When we think about dinosaurs (terrible lizards), we usually visualize huge and fierce animals – they are the ones that have captured our imagination. However, some dinosaurs were actually quite small beasts not much bigger than a chicken. Scuttling about the ground among the giants, small dinosaurs were probably more common than the big ones. Unfortunately, as their bones were so lightweight and their skeletons quite delicate, very few have been preserved as fossils. Nevertheless, a number of good specimens have been found and some of these were preserved in great detail.

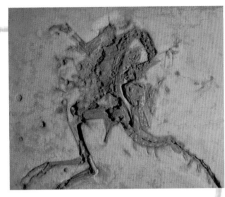

COMPSOGNATHUS SKELETON

Two *Compsognathus* skeletons have been found: one in France, the other in Germany. The German specimen was particularly well-preserved in fine limestone. Not only can we see the skeleton but also the contents of its stomach, showing that its last meal included a small lizard. Some scientists thought *Compsognathus* was the baby of some other type of dinosaur but the blobs scattered around the skeleton are probably eggs, as yet unlaid when the animal died. They prove this *Compsognathus* was an adult female.

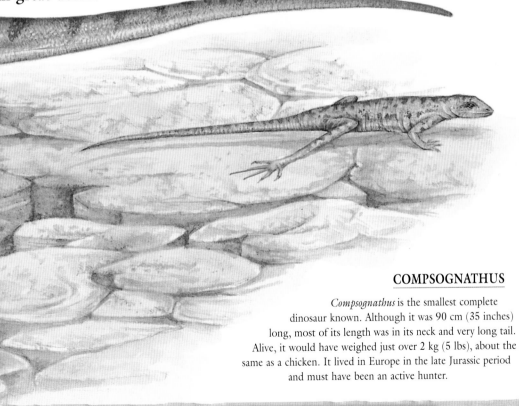

COMPSOGNATHUS

Compsognathus is the smallest complete dinosaur known. Although it was 90 cm (35 inches) long, most of its length was in its neck and very long tail. Alive, it would have weighed just over 2 kg (5 lbs), about the same as a chicken. It lived in Europe in the late Jurassic period and must have been an active hunter.

TRIASSIC 245-208 MYA	EARLY/MID JURASSIC 208-157 MYA	LATE JURASSIC 157-146 MYA	EARLY CRETACEOUS 146-97 MYA	LATE CRETACEOUS 97-65 MYA

A typical *Allosaurus* skull is about a metre (3½ ft) long. The jaws were armed with more than 70 teeth, some measuring 8 cm (3 inches). The teeth were curved, pointed and serrated, ideal for ripping the flesh of large plant-eating dinosaurs. The joints between the skull bones would have allowed the snout to move up and down to help manipulate food. The lower jaws were hinged so they could expand sideways to allow the animal to gulp down big chunks of meat.

JURASSIC GIANT

Some dinosaurs really did live up to their reputation of being enormous fearsome beasts. Probably the most terrifying animal of the late Jurassic period was *Allosaurus*. Its remains have been found in both Tanzania, Africa, and in the sequence of rocks known as the Morrison Formation which stretches down the western United States from the Canadian border to New Mexico. These deposits yielded the most important dinosaur discoveries made in the second half of the nineteenth century. Over a hundred different kinds of dinosaur (mostly plant-eaters) were found there. The most powerful of the meat-eaters found was *Allosaurus*.

MUSCLES

By studying the arrangement of bones in the skeleton and seeing the points of attachment for individual muscles, scientists have worked out what the fleshed-up *Allosaurus* would have looked like. The leg muscles would have allowed it to move at speeds of up to 30 km/h (18 mph) – not particularly swift but fast enough to catch the slow-moving herbivores of the time. The neck muscles would have been massive to control the huge head and powerful jaws.

FEET

The feet of *Allosaurus* had three powerful toes, muscular enough to carry the entire weight of the adult, which must have been over a tonne. Unlike its fingers, the toes were not equipped with hooked claws but with broad hooves that would have helped to bear the great weight. The legs were not particularly long for the size of animal and were evidently not built for speed.

 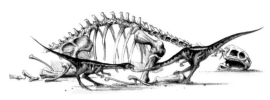

HUNTING

The bones of plant-eaters such as *Camarasaurus* are found throughout the Morrison Formation, often mixed up with the broken teeth of meat-eating dinosaurs. Discoveries like these suggest that the big plant-eaters – especially sick ones – were often attacked and killed by big meat-eaters like *Allosaurus*. Once the killer had eaten its fill, packs of smaller meat-eaters, such as *Ceratosaurus* (*see pages 8-9*), may have scavenged what was left. Anything left over would have been eaten by small animals.

FOREARMS

Allosaurus' hands had three claws: one claw, at 25 cm (10 inches) long, was much larger than the other two. The joint on this first finger allowed the huge claw to turn inwards. *Allosaurus* would have been able to grasp its prey, kill it, then rip it apart. The span of its hand would have been wide enough to grasp the head of an adult man, had there been such a person around in Jurassic times!

ALLOSAURUS IN LIFE

We have a fairly good idea what *Allosaurus* looked like from the thousands of bone specimens (some almost complete skeletons) that have been found. These bones belonged to juveniles that measured about 3 metres (10 ft) from nose to tail-tip, and to adults of about 9 metres (30 ft) long. Some of the *Allosaurus* bones found must have come from 12-metre (40-ft) monsters. Mounted casts of *Allosaurus* skeletons can be seen in many museums around the world. The actual bones are usually kept behind the scenes for research.

TRIASSIC 245-208 MYA	EARLY/MID JURASSIC 208-157 MYA	LATE JURASSIC 157-146 MYA	EARLY CRETACEOUS 146-97 MYA	LATE CRETACEOUS 97-65 MYA

FAST HUNTERS

Back in the late nineteenth/early twentieth century there was a theory that birds and dinosaurs were related. This theory fell out of favour for a long time but was revived in the 1960s when a group of dinosaurs, extremely bird-like in their build, were discovered. They ranged from the size of a goose to the size of a tiger and had wing-like joints in their forearms. They also had strong hind legs with huge, sickle-like killing claws on their feet, showing that they were very fast runners and fierce hunters. These dinosaurs are known as the dromaeosaurids (part of a larger group called the maniraptorans) and are commonly referred to as the 'raptors'.

BIRD OR DROMAEOSAURID?

Right down to the killing claw on its foot *Rahonavis*, an early Cretaceous bird from Madagascar, had the skeleton of a dromaeosaurid. If it had not been for the functional wings, it would have been grouped with the dromaeosaurids.

TERRIBLE CLAWS

The skeleton of a plant-eating *Tenontosaurus*, found in late Cretaceous rocks in Montana, USA, was surrounded by the remains of several *Deinonychus*. This suggests that *Deinonychus* hunted in packs, surrounded a prey animal and then slashed it to death. With its big brain and balancing tail, a *Deinonychus* could have stood on one foot and slashed with the other, or it may have hung on to its prey with its clawed hands and slashed away with both hind feet, as cats do. Before it died, this *Tenontosaurus* must have put up a fight and killed some of its attackers.

UTAHRAPTOR

DEINONYCHUS

VELOCIRAPTOR

BAMBIRAPTOR

A RANGE OF DROMAEOSAURIDS

About the size of a goose, *Bambiraptor* is the smallest of the dromaeosaurids. Turkey-sized *Velociraptor* is probably the best-known. Scientists were first alerted to the bird-like nature of these animals in the 1960s, when tiger-sized *Deinonychus* was discovered. Bigger dromaeosaurids are known but only from bone fragments. *Utahraptor* probably weighed more than a tonne while *Megaraptor* (not shown), known only from a 34-cm (13-inches) killing claw, must have approached the size of the big meat-eaters, such as *Allosaurus* (*see pages 14–15*). Apart from the Argentinian *Megaraptor*, all these animals were found in late Cretaceous rocks in North America.

EARLY BIRD

This fossil of the first bird *Archaeopteryx*, dating from the late Jurassic period, was found in Germany in 1877. If it had not been for the feather impressions in the fossil, the skeleton would have been mistaken for that of a dinosaur because it has a toothed jaw, clawed hands and a long tail. As well as evolving into modern birds, it is possible that some of *Archaeopteryx's* descendants lost their powers of flight and developed into the dromaeosaurids and other related meat-eating dinosaurs of the Cretaceous period. They were certainly closely related to one another.

BAMBIRAPTOR

Any doubts about whether or not dromaeosaurids were related to birds were finally put to rest in the late 1990s, when an almost complete skeleton of *Bambiraptor* was discovered in late Cretaceous rocks in Montana, USA. Every bone seems to be a bird bone, every joint a bird joint. It was no doubt a warm-blooded animal, covered with feathers.

TRIASSIC 245-208 MYA	EARLY/MID JURASSIC 208-157 MYA	LATE JURASSIC 157-146 MYA	EARLY CRETACEOUS 146-97 MYA	LATE CRETACEOUS 97-65 MYA

TROODON

Troodon was one of the maniraptorans, although it was not quite as bird-like as the dromaeosaurids. This small meat-eater of the late Cretaceous period was about 2.5 metres (8 ft) long and may well have had feathers.

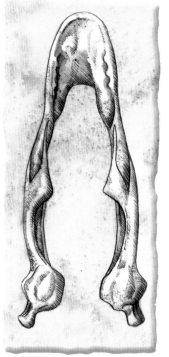

CAENAGNATHUS JAWBONE

Caenagnathus was a dinosaur that probably resembled *Oviraptor*, and may have been an egg eater. Certainly, its toothless lower jaw was quite wide in the middle and would have been good for swallowing eggs. As no other remains have ever been found, *Caenagnathus* remains a bit of a mystery.

OVIRAPTOR HEAD

An *Oviraptor's* head make it easy to believe it might be an egg eater. Its very short, beak-like mouth and its gullet, situated right over the widest part of its jaw, were ideal for swallowing something big and round. As in modern egg-eating snakes, two bones protruding down from its palate were perfectly positioned to tear open an egg on its way down. With its long fingers, just right for grasping eggs, *Oviraptor* may after all have been an egg-eating dinosaur. There seems to have been little else for it to eat on the desert plains of late Cretaceous Mongolia.

EGG THIEF

The jaw of *Caenagnathus* was similar to that of *Chirostenotes*. This was a turkey-sized dinosaur with very long fingers that would have enabled it to raid other dinosaur nests for their eggs. Perhaps there were many different kinds of egg-stealing dinosaurs in late Cretaceous times.

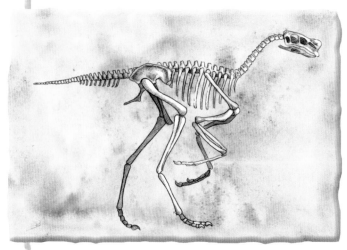

TRIASSIC	EARLY/MID JURASSIC	LATE JURASSIC	EARLY CRETACEOUS	LATE CRETACEOUS
245-208 MYA	208-157 MYA	157-146 MYA	146-97 MYA	97-65 MYA

EGGS & NESTS

Like modern birds, some dinosaurs built nests and laid eggs. The first known dinosaur nests were found by an expedition sent to the Gobi desert from the American Museum of Natural History in 1923. The nests were among remains of herds of the horned dinosaur *Protoceratops*. Alongside the supposed *Protoceratops* eggs lay the skeleton of a toothless meat-eater *Oviraptor*. This so-called 'egg thief' was thought to have been buried in a sandstorm while digging up the eggs. But, as sometimes happens, more evidence caused later palaeontologists to re-evaluate this interpretation.

In the 1990s, another expedition to the Gobi desert found the fossil of an *Oviraptor* sitting on a nest, incubating eggs, which meant those first nests must also have been *Oviraptor* nests!

TROODON EGGS

Fossils of *Troodon* nests show they were oval ridges of mud surrounding the eggs, very much like the nests of *Oviraptor*. The eggs were laid in pairs which suggests that the dinosaur had a pair of oviducts (egg tubes) within its body. A modern bird has only one oviduct. Birds have evolved many such features which keep down their body weight to make flying easier.

NESTING DINOSAUR

In the 1990s, a fossil was found of an *Oviraptor* sitting on a nest with its arms spread protectively around some eggs, evidently keeping them warm with the heat of its body. Modern birds do this efficiently as their feathers provide excellent insulation. This is one of the indirect lines of evidence that suggests that *Oviraptor*, and many other bird-like dinosaurs, had feathers.

BIRD OR DINOSAUR?

As well as finding the first dinosaur nests, the American expeditions to the Gobi desert in the 1920s uncovered many other dinosaur remains. One of these we now call *Mononykus* was a total puzzle. Was it a bird or was it a dinosaur? If it was a bird, its arms were too short for it to fly. If it was a dinosaur, what good were hands reduced to a single finger with a big claw? In the 1980s, when new specimens were found, *Mononykus* was found to have belonged to a group of related animals, the alvarezsaurids – a distinct group within the maniraptorans – that ranged from South America to Central Asia. Today, we still do not know whether they were birds or dinosaurs.

MONONYKUS

The best known and most complete of the alvarezsaurids was *Mononykus*. It looked like a very lightly-built, meat-eating dinosaur with spindly legs and a long tail. The two forelimbs are remarkable. They are short and have a shelf of bone, which in modern birds would support wing feathers, and each bears a single stout, stubby claw. These forelimbs probably evolved from the functional wings of a flying ancestor, such as the late Jurassic *Archaeopteryx*.

OSTRICH

One function of non-flying wings in modern running birds is for display. The ostrich makes a big show of its wing feathers when it is courting a mate or threatening an enemy. It is quite possible that the part-bird/part-dinosaur animals of the Cretaceous period also had flamboyant feathers on their flightless wings and used them for display. Unfortunately, such behaviour cannot be proven by fossil evidence.

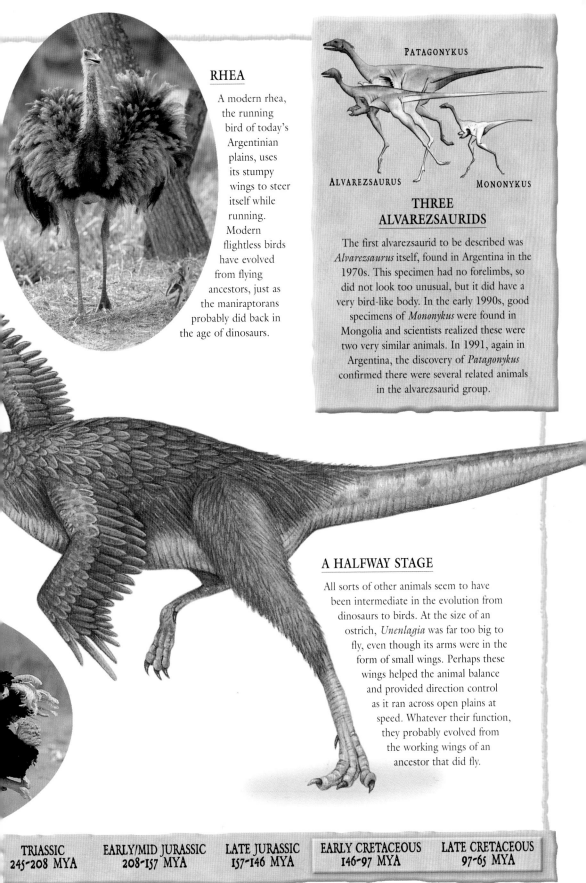

RHEA

A modern rhea, the running bird of today's Argentinian plains, uses its stumpy wings to steer itself while running. Modern flightless birds have evolved from flying ancestors, just as the maniraptorans probably did back in the age of dinosaurs.

PATAGONYKUS

ALVAREZSAURUS

MONONYKUS

THREE ALVAREZSAURIDS

The first alvarezsaurid to be described was *Alvarezsaurus* itself, found in Argentina in the 1970s. This specimen had no forelimbs, so did not look too unusual, but it did have a very bird-like body. In the early 1990s, good specimens of *Mononykus* were found in Mongolia and scientists realized these were two very similar animals. In 1991, again in Argentina, the discovery of *Patagonykus* confirmed there were several related animals in the alvarezsaurid group.

A HALFWAY STAGE

All sorts of other animals seem to have been intermediate in the evolution from dinosaurs to birds. At the size of an ostrich, *Unenlagia* was far too big to fly, even though its arms were in the form of small wings. Perhaps these wings helped the animal balance and provided direction control as it ran across open plains at speed. Whatever their function, they probably evolved from the working wings of an ancestor that did fly.

TRIASSIC 245-208 MYA	EARLY/MID JURASSIC 208-157 MYA	LATE JURASSIC 157-146 MYA	EARLY CRETACEOUS 146-97 MYA	LATE CRETACEOUS 97-65 MYA

TERRIBLE HAND

An intriguing fossil from late Cretaceous rocks in Mongolia shows a pair of arms, 2.5 metres (8 ft) long, with three-clawed hands. The animal has been given the name *Deinocheirus* but we know nothing else about it. The bones look as if they are from an ornithomimid but they are far bigger than those of any known member of this group. For now, the owner of these extraordinary bones remains a mystery.

GALLIMIMUS SKELETON

Gallimimus is probably the best known of the Ornithomimids. It had a small toothless beak, which it used for cropping fruit and vegetation. This dinosaur was built for speed, and could run at up to 80 km/h (50 mph), as fast as a race horse. It usually paced around slowly, stalking small mammals or snapping up seeds and insects, but its speed meant that it could escape from most predators. Its long tail acted as a counterbalance to the front of the body, propelling it forward while it sprinted. Its hipbone also pointed forward. This skeleton is mounted on display at the Natural History Museum in London.

STRUTHIOMIMUS

ORNITHOMIMIDS

All ornithomimids looked similar but varied somewhat in size. *Struthiomimus* was about the size of an ostrich. *Pelecanimimus* was one of the earliest. It had a pouch of skin beneath its long jaws, which had hundreds of tiny teeth in them. This suggests the teeth of the group became smaller and smaller before disappearing altogether in the later ornithomimids. *Garidumimus*, named after a mythical Hindu bird, had a small crest on its head. The biggest known was *Gallimimus*, the 'chicken mimic', at 4–5 metres (13–16 ft) long. Some chicken!

TRIASSIC 245-208 MYA	EARLY/MID JURASSIC 208-157 MYA	LATE JURASSIC 157-146 MYA	EARLY CRETACEOUS 146-97 MYA	LATE CRETACEOUS 97-65 MYA

BIRD MIMICS

 One group of dinosaurs has always been thought to look very much like birds. Ornithomimids (bird mimics) had plump, compact bodies; big eyes; toothless beaks on small heads that were supported on long, slender necks, and long running legs with thick muscles close to the hip. Typical of the group was a dinosaur called *Struthiomimus* (ostrich mimic) from the late Cretaceous period. Although they fall into the category of meat-eating dinosaurs and would have descended from purely carnivorous ancestors, these dinosaurs were probably omnivorous, eating fruit and leaves as well as insects and small vertebrates, such as lizards. Ostriches and other ground birds of today are also omnivores.

BUILT FOR SPEED

As with most meat-eating dinosaurs the skeleton of an ornithomimid, such as this *ornithomimus*, is very bird-like. Its head would have been held farther forward than that of an ostrich, balanced by its long tail. However, they had very similar legs with a very short femur (thighbone) that would have held all the muscles so that the lower leg and the toes were worked only by tendons. This gives a very lightweight leg that could move quickly – a running leg.

GALLIMIMUS

GARIDUMIMUS

PELECANIMIMUS

EMU

A modern emu is a typical plains-living animal. The keen eyes in the head, held high on the top of a long neck, are able to spot danger coming from a long way away across the open spaces. The strong running legs are then able to take the bird out of danger at great speed. Because of the physical similarity, we think that the ornithomimids of the late Cretaceous period had a similar lifestyle on the open plains of North America and central Asia.

ERLIKOSAURUS SKULL

The best known segnosaurid skull is that of *Erlikosaurus*. It looks very much like the skulls of some of the big plant-eating dinosaurs. Behind its toothless beak the teeth are small and leaf-shaped. Some scientists have suggested this might be the skull of a fish-eating dinosaur and that the foot bones (which are also unusual) could have been webbed for swimming. However, the rest of the skeleton suggests that it could not have been a swimming animal.

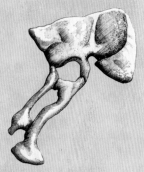

SEGNOSAURUS HIPBONE

The hipbones of meat-eating dinosaurs are usually quite distinctive. The pubis bone at the front points forwards. In the segnosaurids, the pubis bone sweeps backwards. This is usually only seen in plant-eating dinosaurs, as it gives more space for the big plant-eating guts that such animals need. It would have given the body of this dinosaur a very dumpy appearance. This is part of what makes the whole group a puzzle.

SEGNOSAURIDS

Sometimes, part of a skeleton is so unlike any known dinosaur, nobody knows what kind it is. Such is the case with segnosaurids. In the 1920s, the first bones, found in late Cretaceous rocks in Mongolia, were thought to be from a giant turtle, but were re-classified as dinosaur remains in the 1970s. The various bits of bone were all so unalike they seemed to be from different families of dinosaur. Even now, the name therizinosaurid is sometimes used for the group; the name was first used as the original classification of the forelimb, as opposed to segnosaurid, the name set up when the skull and backbone were studied. These dinosaurs were thought to be meat-eaters; then to be prosauropods, one of the long-necked plant-eaters. They are back with the meat-eaters for the time being.

A MODERN PARALLEL

The anteater is a modern animal with claws that seem too big for its body. It uses them to rip through the tough walls of anthills to get at the living chambers of the ant colony. Some scientists have suggested that this is how the segnosaurids lived, while others doubt this diet could have supported such a big animal.

TRIASSIC 245-208 MYA	EARLY/MID JURASSIC 208-157 MYA	LATE JURASSIC 157-146 MYA	EARLY CRETACEOUS 146-97 MYA	LATE CRETACEOUS 97-65 MYA

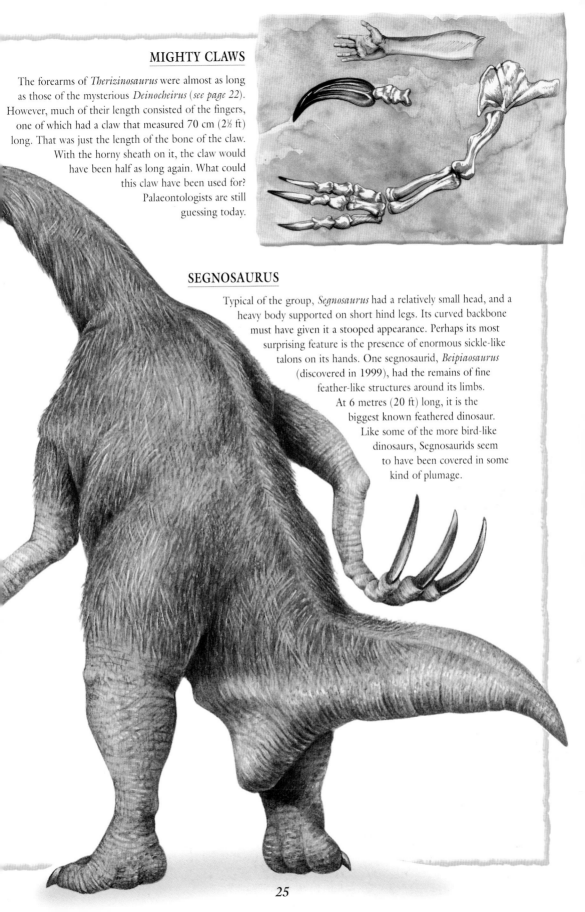

MIGHTY CLAWS

The forearms of *Therizinosaurus* were almost as long as those of the mysterious *Deinocheirus* (*see page 22*). However, much of their length consisted of the fingers, one of which had a claw that measured 70 cm (2½ ft) long. That was just the length of the bone of the claw. With the horny sheath on it, the claw would have been half as long again. What could this claw have been used for? Palaeontologists are still guessing today.

SEGNOSAURUS

Typical of the group, *Segnosaurus* had a relatively small head, and a heavy body supported on short hind legs. Its curved backbone must have given it a stooped appearance. Perhaps its most surprising feature is the presence of enormous sickle-like talons on its hands. One segnosaurid, *Beipiaosaurus* (discovered in 1999), had the remains of fine feather-like structures around its limbs. At 6 metres (20 ft) long, it is the biggest known feathered dinosaur. Like some of the more bird-like dinosaurs, Segnosaurids seem to have been covered in some kind of plumage.

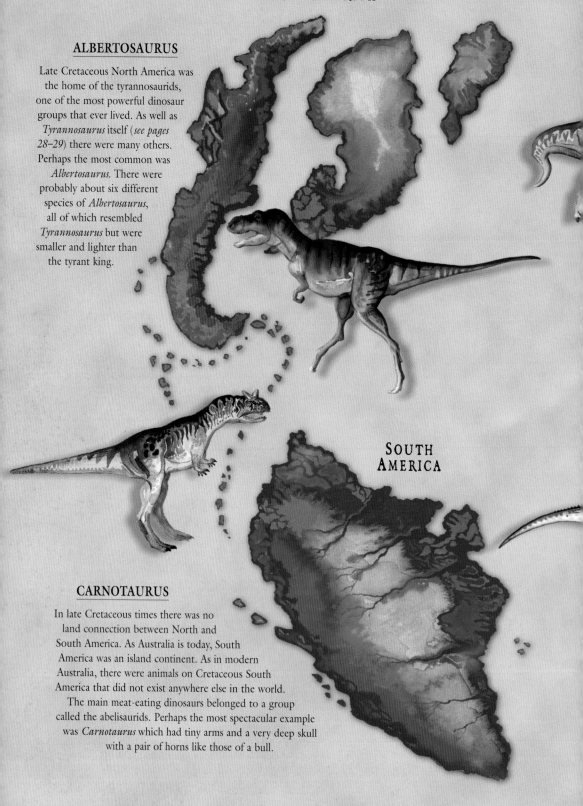

ALBERTOSAURUS

Late Cretaceous North America was the home of the tyrannosaurids, one of the most powerful dinosaur groups that ever lived. As well as *Tyrannosaurus* itself (*see pages 28–29*) there were many others. Perhaps the most common was *Albertosaurus*. There were probably about six different species of *Albertosaurus*, all of which resembled *Tyrannosaurus* but were smaller and lighter than the tyrant king.

SOUTH AMERICA

CARNOTAURUS

In late Cretaceous times there was no land connection between North and South America. As Australia is today, South America was an island continent. As in modern Australia, there were animals on Cretaceous South America that did not exist anywhere else in the world.

The main meat-eating dinosaurs belonged to a group called the abelisaurids. Perhaps the most spectacular example was *Carnotaurus* which had tiny arms and a very deep skull with a pair of horns like those of a bull.

LATE CRETACEOUS ISOLATION

Early in the dinosaur age, there was only one landmass (*see page 7*). All continents of the world were part of a single supercontinent called Pangaea. It took 150 million years for Pangaea to break up into most of the continents we know today. At the beginning of the dinosaur age, the same kinds of dinosaurs existed all over the world. But the Earth's surface was splitting apart as rift valleys opened up into seas and then into oceans. Animals then began to evolve in different ways. By the end of the dinosaur age, there were still meat eaters on each continent, but they were no longer closely related to those on other landmasses.

EUROPE

ASIA

AFRICA

MADAGASCAR

TARBOSAURUS

The Bering Strait did not exist at all at the beginning of the age of dinosaurs. North America was joined to Asia by a broad neck of land that extended westwards from Alaska, and very similar animals lived on both continents. The main big meat-eaters in Asia were also tyrannosaurids. *Albertosaurus* did not reach into Asia. Instead, Asia supported tyrannosaurids of its own. The biggest, *Tarbosaurus*, was very like North America's *Tyrannosaurus*.

DELTADROMEUS

On the continent of Africa the biggest of the meat-eaters (*see Carcharodontosaurus, pages 30–31*) were evolved from animals close to *Allosaurus* (*see pages 14–15*). However, there were a number of others such as *Deltadromeus* which had evolved from the small meat-eaters – the coelurosaurids – of the Jurassic period.

MAJUNGATHOLUS

The big meat-eating dinosaur found on the island of Madagascar was *Majungatholus*. It is odd that it was an abelisaurid, like the meat-eaters of South America and India. This means that before the continents split up, South America, Madagascar and India were joined together for long enough for abelisaurid's ancestors to migrate across all three continents while they were still attached to Antarctica and after Africa had drifted away (abelisaurids are not commonly found in Africa).

TRIASSIC 245-208 MYA	EARLY/MID JURASSIC 208-157 MYA	LATE JURASSIC 157-146 MYA	EARLY CRETACEOUS 146-97 MYA	LATE CRETACEOUS 97-65 MYA

FOOTPRINT

In the late 1980s, a dinosaur footprint almost a metre (3 ft) long was discovered on a slab of late Cretaceous rock in New Mexico. Whatever beast made it had a meat-eater's claws. There was only one print, so the stride of the animal must have been greater than the almost 3-metre (10-ft) long slab of rock. Scientists estimate the animal was moving at 8–10 km/h (5–6 mph). We cannot be sure this footprint was made by *Tyrannosaurus*, but we know of no bigger meat-eating dinosaurs in Cretaceous America.

TYRANNOSAURIDS

At 12 metres (39 ft) long and 6 metres (20 ft) tall, *Tyrannosaurus* must have been the scourge of the North American continent at the end of the dinosaur age. So far, about 15 specimens of *Tyrannosaurus* have been discovered in various states of completeness. From these we have built up a picture of what the mighty beasts looked like. However, there is still much debate about how they lived. Some scientists think they actively hunted, perhaps waiting in ambush for duckbills, the big plant-eaters of the time, then charging out at them from the cover of the forest. Others insist they were too big for such activity but would have scavenged carrion, the meat of already-dead animals. Maybe they did both.

A RANGE OF TYRANNOSAURIDS

Daspletosaurus from North America was similar to *Tyrannosaurus* but was a little smaller and had a heavy head with fewer but larger teeth. At about 6 metres (20 ft) long, *Alioramus* was a medium-sized tyrannosaurid from Asia. It had a long skull with knobbles and spikes along the top. The smallest was *Nanotyrannus*, from Montana, USA, which was about 4 metres (13 ft) long. Experts are undecided about this last one. Some think it may have been a small *Albertosaurus*, but the one skull available to study was certainly from an adult animal.

NANOTYRANNUS

FRIGHTFUL BITE

Tyrannosaurus had incredibly powerful jaws and teeth used to rip flesh from its prey. Gouges in the pelvic bone of a late Cretaceous specimen of the three-horned dinosaur *Triceratops* exactly match the size and spacing of the teeth of *Tyrannosaurus*. From these marks scientists could tell that a *Tyrannosaurus* bit down into the meat of the hind leg and tore it away from the bone when the *Triceratops* was already dead. But whether or not it was the *Tyrannosaurus* that killed it, nobody can tell.

TYRANT LIZARD KING

Tyrannosaurus, the biggest of the tyrannosaurids, is often known by its full species name *Tyrannosaurus rex* or simply *T. rex*. Other dinosaurs also have full species names, such as *Allosaurus atrox*, *Velociraptor mongoliensis* and so on, but these are usually only used by scientists.

DASPLETOSAURUS

ALIORAMUS

COPROLITE

Fossilized animal droppings are known to geologists as coprolites and they give useful clues to an extinct animal's diet. But, as with footprints, it is often impossible to tell what animal made which coprolite. Big coprolites, more than 20 cm (8 inches) long, that may have come from *Tyrannosaurus*, have been found to contain smashed-up undigested bone fragments.

TRIASSIC 245-208 MYA	EARLY/MID JURASSIC 208-157 MYA	LATE JURASSIC 157-146 MYA	EARLY CRETACEOUS 146-97 MYA	LATE CRETACEOUS 97-65 MYA

MONSTROUS SKULL

The skull of *Carcharodontosaurus* is almost completely known. When putting the skull bones together the scientists only had to recreate the missing front of the snout and the bones at the very rear. This they could do by drawing on their knowledge of other skulls. The final skull is 1.5 metres (5 ft) long and had strong, curved, shark-like teeth. We know far less about the skull of *Giganotosaurus*. What we can be sure of is that the jaws were not as powerful as those of *Tyrannosaurus*, the teeth were not as strong and it had an even smaller brain than the Tyrant Lizard King.

CARCHARODONTOSAURUS

Related to the Jurassic *Allosaurus* (*see pages 14–15*) *Carcharodontosaurus* came from Morocco, Africa. Some fossils of it were first discovered by a German expedition in 1925 but they were destroyed when their museum was bombed during World War II, along with the original remains of *Spinosaurus* found on the same expedition. Only when more fossils were discovered in the mid–1990s did palaeontologists realize that *Carcharodontosaurus* was a giant 15 metres (50 ft) long.

TRIASSIC 245-208 MYA	EARLY/MID JURASSIC 208-157 MYA	LATE JURASSIC 157-146 MYA	EARLY CRETACEOUS 146-97 MYA	LATE CRETACEOUS 97-65 MYA

THE NEW KINGS

What was the biggest, strongest and fiercest meat-eating dinosaur that ever lived? *Tyrannosaurus*? Not any more! For the past hundred years we have said that *Tyrannosaurus* was the most powerful of the meat-eating dinosaurs. Generations of scientists have believed this to be so and have even stated that it would be mechanically impossible for bigger meat-eating animals to have existed. But now, the remains of even bigger meat-eaters are being found. In the 1990s, the skeletons of two carnivorous dinosaurs were found within a year of one another: one in South America, the other in Africa. Although neither skeleton was complete, they appear to have belonged to a group of dinosaurs that were even longer than *Tyrannosaurus*.

TYRANNOSAURUS

CARCHARODONTOSAURUS

GIGANOTOSAURUS

COMPARING KINGS

Both *Carcharodontosaurus* and *Giganotosaurus* were longer than the previous record-holder *Tyrannosaurus*. However, as shown above only *Tyrannosaurus* is known from complete skeletons and there is still a lot we don't know about the other two. Even so, *Tyrannosaurus* seems to have been a much heavier animal and was higher at the hip, so we could still say that the biggest meat-eating dinosaur that is completely known is *Tyrannosaurus*. Still the king!

GIGANOTOSAURUS

The great meat-eating dinosaur *Giganotosaurus* seems to have been closely related to *Carcharodontosaurus*, even though it lived in isolated South America in the late Cretaceous period while the other lived in Africa. It is likely that in the early part of the Cretaceous period, before the continents were separated by oceans, the ancestors of these animals spread across the whole world. After the continents split apart, *Giganotosaurus* began to evolve separately.

DID YOU KNOW?

It is very unusual for a dinosaur to form a fossil. Fossils are nearly always of water-living animals. The rocks in which fossils are found are formed from sediment that builds up on the beds of seas, lakes, rivers and sometimes deserts. When a land animal dies, it is scavenged by meat-eating animals, the skeleton is pulled to bits and what is left is nibbled away by insects or rotted by bacteria. If a dinosaur was to become a fossil, its body would have to fall into water and immediately be buried in sediment where nothing could reach it.

We only know of about a fifth of the dinosaur species that ever lived. It would be very difficult for a dinosaur living in an upland forest or mountain slopes ever to become fossilized. Looking at the variety of animals and their range of habitats today, scientists have estimated there were probably somewhere between 1,200 and 1,500 different dinosaur species. We know of about 300 of them.

We do not know whether or not any dinosaur climbed trees. Tree-living animals tend not to become fossils. The trees may be a long way from the sea or anywhere that fossils may form. Also, tree-living animals are lightweight with delicate skeletons, likely to break easily. However, some scientists think maniraptorans developed their curved claws to climb tree trunks and hang on to branches. The huge claws of *Deinocheirus* (*see page 22*) have even been interpreted as having come from a gigantic sloth-like climbing dinosaur. This is all speculation, however.

Despite all the evidence some scientists still doubt that birds evolved from dinosaurs. They believe that they evolved from the same crocodile-like ancestors that gave rise to the dinosaurs themselves and that the two lines diverged back in Triassic times. But most scientists now think the dinosaurs did not become extinct 65 million years ago – they just grew feathers and flew away!

We nearly didn't have the word 'dinosaur'. In 1832, the German palaeontologist Herman von Meyer was the first scientist to try to put these newly-discovered animals in their own classification. He called them the 'pachypodes'. Sir Richard Owen's classification of the 'dinosauria' set up nine years later became the accepted one.

ACKNOWLEDGEMENTS

We would like to thank: Helen Wire, www.fossilfinds.com and Elizabeth Wiggans for their assistance. Illustrations by John Alston, Lisa Alderson, Dougal Dixon, Simon Mendez and Luis Rey.
Copyright © 2004 **ticktock** Publishing Ltd.
First published in Great Britain by ticktock Publishing Ltd., Unit 2, Orchard Business Centre, North Farm Road, Tunbridge Wells, Kent TN2 3XF.
All rights reserved. No part of this publication may be reproduced, stored in a retrieval system, or transmitted in any form or by any means electronic, mechanical, photocopying, recording or otherwise, without prior written permission of the copyright owner.
A CIP catalogue record for this book is available from the British Library. ISBN 1 86007 508 8 (paperback).

Picture Credits:
t=top, b=bottom, c=centre, l=left, r=right, OFC=outside front cover, IFC=inside front cover, IBC=inside back cover, OBC=outside back cover

Lisa Alderson: 2bl, 2/3c, 10/11c, 17t, 20l, 21c, 25c, 31br. John Alston: 2tl, 6/7c, 7t, 12t, 12b, 14tl, 15t, 18cl, 18bl, 21tr, 24tl, 24bl, 25tr, 26/27, 28tl. Corbis: 6tl, 9b, 20b, 21tr, 23tr, 23br, 24cb. Dougal Dixon: 3b, 4b, 8b, 9tl, 9tr, 17b, 31tr. Fossil Finds: 2cl, 12c, 19tr, 29br. Dr Peter Griffith: 13t, 17c. Simon Mendez: OFC, 6/7b, 8c, 10-11c, 14/15c, 15b, 16b, 16/17c, 18tl, 22/23c, 29cr, 30c, 32cr, OBCl, OBCcr, OBCb. OBCcl. Natural History Museum: 7cr, 10tl, 29t. Oxford City Museum: 4tl, 4c, 4tr. Planet Earth Pictures: 10bl. Luis Rey: 19c, 28/29c. Paul Sereno: 3cr, 30tr.

Every effort has been made to trace the copyright holders and we apologize in advance for any unintentional omissions. We would be pleased to insert the appropriate acknowledgement in any subsequent edition of this publication.

snapping-turtle
guide